A Counterintuitive Code for Resilience
During Disruption and Change

Hacking
Uncertainty

PRICE PRITCHETT, PH.D.

forward
forward
forward
forward
"There is always a way to move forward."
forward
forward
forward
forward

—Julia Cameron

Printed in the United States of America

ISBN 978-0-944002-49-0

Introduction

Change...

Sometimes you can see it coming.
Other times you just get a feeling inside,
    the vague sense that something big,
        something different is coming down.
But now and then it takes you totally by surprise.

Regardless of how it approaches, though, change
usually comes with a traveling companion:

Uncertainty.

This uncertainty often blankets us well before the actual changes arrive. Like a descending fog that marks a shift in weather, uncertainty reduces visibility into the future, blurs the situation at hand, and raises a whole new set of questions.

Moving through this field of ambiguity, you may be tempted to insist on clarity. . . to demand solid answers . . . to push toward closure. Or, let's put it differently: You might be intent on "managing" the uncertainty—you know, determined to eliminate it, to force it out of your life and career.

That's not likely to be a winning strategy.

The defining feature of uncertainty is its very unmanageability. Seeking to control it is like trying to rearrange fog. What *is* manageable, and what you should focus on, is managing *you*. That is where your power lies, because that is what you're free to control.

We are all the product of chance and choice. Working in tandem with circumstances that life puts before us, we choose our moves, and so become co-designers of our future.

Hacking Uncertainty maps for you the "road less traveled," a secret route through disruption and change, providing a shortcut that helps you move through today's fog of uncertainty toward the best possible outcomes.

You'll learn the unusual psychology of dealing with unpredictability, a counterintuitive code for managing yourself under conditions of low visibility and high stakes.

The program spelled out in the following pages probably isn't what you would expect. It also may feel unnatural to you. But it's powerful, and you can make it work.

Beware of
Your Natural Impulses.

As change closes in and uncertainty clouds the future, a primal alarm goes off deep inside your brain. Without any conscious effort on your part, this basic survival instinct warns you: "Be careful!" Automatically you start scanning for danger.

This natural impulse, designed purely for your self-defense, asks questions like these:

- How could I get hurt in this deal?
- What do I stand to lose?
- Where could things go wrong?
- What should I do to protect myself?

These are good questions, evidence that this instinct has your best interests at heart. But while it's good at spotting the potential for harm, it cannot detect the glint of opportunity. Good possibilities get ignored.

With no eye for the potential upside of change, this particular instinct conducts a one-sided risk assessment, focusing only on protecting you from something negative. The hazard? It can distract you from seeing the positive aspects of change.

And there's another funny thing about us humans that you should know: We're wired such that we just naturally weigh losses differently than gains. It's like we use different scales. Dr. Daniel Kahneman, a psychologist, won the Nobel Prize in Economics for his research that discovered this peculiar behavior. He found that losses carry twice as much psychological impact as wins. No surprise, then, that when we survey uncertain situations, our attention focuses mostly on dodging the threats. This negative bias interferes with the ability to see opportunity and stifles our willingness to take promising risks.

Your challenge is to think past these natural impulses. What if the uncertainty just happens to be giftwrapping, and your job is to find what's hidden inside?

 Not everything that is bad comes to hurt us.
—Italian proverb

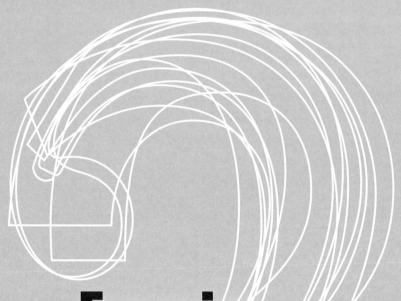

Examine Your Tolerance for Ambiguity.

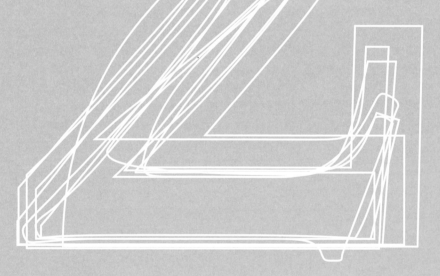

Many people find ambiguity and uncertainty more difficult to deal with than change itself. How do you stack up on this personality trait?

People with a low tolerance for ambiguity like for their world to be systematic, orderly, and predictable. Give them a map, a schedule, a plan . . . the more structure, the better. The fuzzier the situation—that is, the more they have to deal with unknowns and a lack of clarity—the more bothersome it becomes. When forced to wait for answers, wondering how things will turn out, the vagueness gnaws at them and they get itchy to bring about resolution. Closure becomes the top priority. Trouble is, in attempting to drive out ambiguity and improve their psychological comfort level, they often complicate matters and compromise their position. Patience might have produced much better options.

In contrast, people with a high tolerance for ambiguity find it much easier to handle the open-endedness of uncertainty. They're comfortable feeling their way along . . . giving the situation time to unfold . . . letting it teach them how to proceed. They're willing to improvise and deal with reality as it arrives. This keeps them open to possibilities and positions them to maneuver toward opportunity.

So which way do you lean? On a 10-point scale—with 1 being very low tolerance for ambiguity, and 10 representing extreme comfort with ambiguity—where would you score? Seriously think about it. Now circle the number that you think fits:

```
        1    2    3    4    5    6    7    8    9    10
LOW  |  <------------------------------------------>  |  HIGH
```

Joe Louis, the legendary boxer, said, "Everyone has a plan until they've been hit." The lower your score, the harder the punch when uncertainty takes a swing at you.

Here's the thing to remember: Your tolerance for ambiguity will color your view of the situation at hand and predispose you to react a certain way. But you're still the person in charge of you.

 Wanting to know where we are going is often how we fail to go anywhere at all.

—Julia Cameron

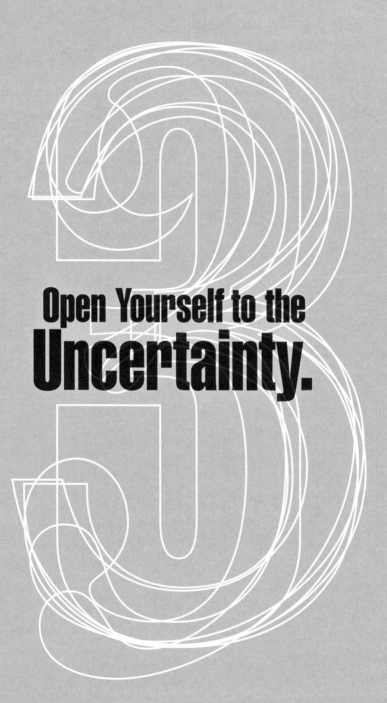

Open Yourself to the
Uncertainty.

You're probably telling yourself that you'd prefer for things to be *decided*, squared away and settled, so you can know what you'll be dealing with in the days ahead.

But, wait! That same kind of "knowing" is what you *thought* you had before this uncertain situation developed, right? Turns out what you had was fake certainty—like counterfeit money—and you were just deceiving yourself. We do this all the time.

Fact is, life doesn't give any of us reliable currency regarding the certainty of our future. We cruise along nursing a broad range of expectations, feeling pretty wealthy with predictability, while most of the so-called certainty that we carry around inside us is actually phony. Frankly, we're pretty much broke when it comes to knowing for sure what life is bringing our way.

The future is always a crapshoot. Let's accept that. And let's open ourselves to this uncertainty as it blankets our lives.

Instead of merely focusing on defensive measures, why not embrace uncertainty? Rather than pulling back, playing it safe, or taking a passive wait-and-see approach, why not decide to wait-and-do? Look at this as a unique opportunity to alter the angle of your life and bend it in the direction of your wants. Allow it to unfreeze your thinking and introduce you to better possibilities.

The big questions here are: "What can *you* do now? Will you accept personal accountability for what comes next? How can you create fire by rubbing these sticks of uncertainty together?"

 The quest for certainty blocks the search for meaning. Uncertainty is the very condition to impel man to unfold his powers.

—Erich Fromm

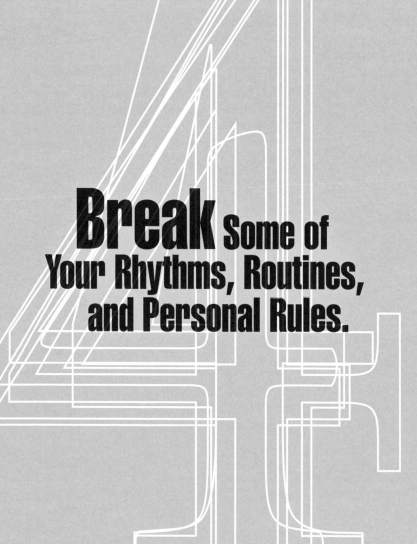

Break Some of Your Rhythms, Routines, and Personal Rules.

People often try to cope with uncertainty by retreating. Confronted with a lot of unknowns, they shrink away from the unpredictability, seeking the comfort and perceived safety of their old habits. They want to feel more grounded—better stabilized—so they move toward the familiar in their pursuit of equilibrium.

Wrong direction.

This simply isn't the time to cling to the past or to hunker down in your same old sameness. Don't get stuck in your pre-existing mindset and behavior patterns. Look, uncertainty is offering something new. Don't run from it. Instead of becoming more set in your ways, you need to loosen up. Rather than stiffening yourself against the unknown, you should relax a bit and start coloring outside the lines of your usual life.

One of the best antidotes for uncertainty is to deliberately bring more newness into your world—more, well, unfamiliarity. You need to be proactive and self-directed, not reactive and retreating. So move beyond your habitual box. Give yourself permission to try new things, feel new feelings, and consider your life from new angles.

You can start with little things. Take a different and unusual route to work. Choose new magazines, TV programs, and restaurants. Change the sequence in how you go about your job. Hang out with some different people. Maybe visit a different state or country.

I know—these sound like utterly trivial changes. But it's our mundane habits that keep us caged. Our unspoken personal rules and commonplace routines govern most of what we think and do in our everyday life. Think you'd prefer to stretch your boundaries with a bigger challenge? Fine, choose your drama. If you want to go hang-gliding or climb the Himalayas, have at it.

The idea here is to give yourself new sensory experiences . . . new connections . . . fresh perspectives . . . plus, most importantly, new insights into who you really are and how you want to live into the future.

The secret is to deal with uncertainty on its own terms.

 To practice the art of uncertainty is to get comfortable with being 'out of control.'
—Dennis Merritt Jones

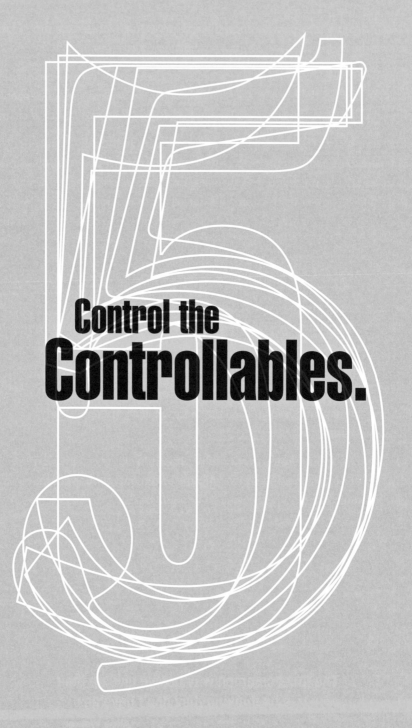

Control the
Controllables.

Want to know the most common mistake in dealing with uncertainty? Hands down, the main foul-up is people mismanaging *themselves*.

One of the best examples of this mistake is when people try to control things that are beyond their reach. This happens when we seek to run other people's lives, or when we struggle to change circumstances that aren't ours to change. It's a frustrating, spirit-killing exercise, but you'll be tempted to try.

People also mismanage themselves to the other extreme, like when they forfeit their ability to steer themselves through the unknowns. Feeling vulnerable and assuming helplessness, they abdicate their power, resigning themselves to the winds of chance. Naturally, this passivity invites even more drift into their lives. In fact, you might ask yourself how much of the uncertainty you're feeling these days is actually caused by *you*—e.g., could part of it be your own lack of commitment, unclear intention, a shortage of initiative, or unwillingness to risk?

Just remember, your big controllable is you. Focus there. You're the person in charge of your attitude, your thinking, your behavior—that's all you—and you're the one who must maneuver yourself through the uncertainty.

You can decide to curl up in a fetal position and cry. You could choose to be angry and go throw rocks at cars. You're free to resign from reality and lose yourself in wishful thinking. You can drive yourself crazy trying to read the end of this uncertainty story that's yet to be written.

Or, another option: You can stay fully present in the moment—explore the mystery of this *nowness*—and live into the uncertainty with everything you've got. It's your call.

 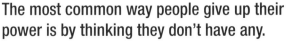 **The most common way people give up their power is by thinking they don't have any.**
—Alice Walker

Focus
on Contributing.

Uncertainty does two things that are especially problematic. First, it prompts us to become overly preoccupied with our own personal needs and concerns. Second, it can cause us to reduce our investment in the situation at hand, withholding ourselves as a means of self-protection or because we just decide not to care as much as before.

Both of these reactions work to our disadvantage.

The more self-absorbed you become, the more likely it is that uncertainty will prey on you. Sure, it makes sense to look out for old #1. But when you're consumed with your own wants and needs, you lose touch with others who are involved in the uncertainty equation. This kind of self-centeredness is the opposite of what *now* is calling for. Try to redirect your attention—get outside yourself—and be mindful of other people's needs.

Next, fight the impulse to sideline yourself, to care less, or to be non-giving. Withholding yourself will most likely only weaken your position. If you're wanting to dilute the uncertainty, think in terms of what you might contribute to others or to the situation in general. Spend freely of yourself. Give more than would be expected. Produce evidence that you're someone who makes a valuable difference.

Uncertainty feeds on idleness and inertia. So it pays to be productive . . . to invest yourself fully in the situation . . . to be passionate with generosity. That will serve you far better than obsessing about what's missing and what seems hard or unfair.

Contributing. It's an enabling approach for dealing with uncertainty and, frankly, you will be the main beneficiary. It will validate you and strengthen your sense of self.

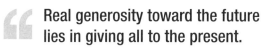

Real generosity toward the future lies in giving all to the present.

—Albert Camus

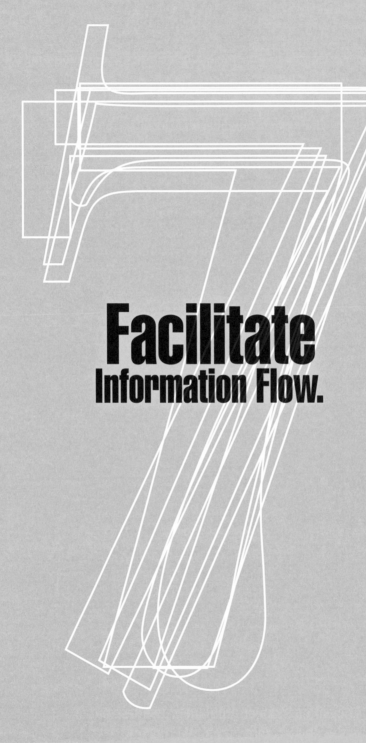

Facilitate
Information Flow.

So often we ourselves add to the fog of uncertainty by communicating too cautiously.

For example, let's say you feel unsure about the situation and somewhat at risk. So you bottle up your feelings and thoughts, carefully screening what you say in order to feel "safer." Trouble is, the more you go quiet or edit your words, the more it triggers reticence in others. Your reserve naturally makes them more tentative. Guardedness is highly contagious, so the information vacuum just keeps growing.

Look, uncertainty likes to live in the dark. It thrives on sketchy understanding, open questions, and incomplete data. Do you really want to feed the beast?

If you crave a fuller understanding of what's going on, why not take a few more communication risks? Start by considering how *you* might open up, how revealing more of your ideas and feelings could reduce the ambiguity. If you have the guts to be a little more authentic, a little more forthcoming, will the next person reciprocate? Will you take that gamble?

You can decide against self-disclosure, but don't kid yourself—you're still throwing the dice. In fact, trying to play it safe often poses the bigger risk. The more communication dries up, the more you're going on guesswork. And that just means even more uncertainty.

You'll be most effective at facilitating information flow if you go face-to-face. That gives you the most data to work with because you get to process more than mere words. You get the non-verbal communication, the body language, which often carries the most important messages.

So take your best shot: Get next to the person, then open up.

 The single biggest problem in communication is the illusion that it has taken place.

—George Bernard Shaw

Follow the Rules of Improv.

Maneuvering through uncertainty is like performing on an improv comedy stage. You're going into the situation unscripted and unrehearsed. It's hard to predict what will happen next. You have to ad lib and take it as it comes.

Since you'll be winging it—making it up as you go along—you need to learn some of the basic techniques for improv. Fact is, the professionals who are great at improv comedy follow a set of strict guidelines. Their performance is not as random as you might think.

Here are the top ten rules according to the masters of improv. These same fundamentals provide a strategy for performing spontaneously and being effective in the *nowness* you encounter.

1. Go with whatever the other performer (or perhaps the world) throws at you. Your job is to make whatever is happening in the moment work. Agree to the basic situation and setup. Say, "Yes, and . . ."
2. After the "and," give new information to your partner. Avoid questions.
3. Don't block, negate, or deny anything in a scene.
4. Focus on the here and now, what's going on right at this moment. Listen, watch, and concentrate.
5. Work to the top of your intelligence.
6. Make actional choices—that is, choices which forward the action in a scene.
7. Avoid judging what is going down except in terms of whether it needs help.
8. Your prime responsibility is to support. Watch the other person's back.
9. Trust one another to do the right thing.
10. Always be changed by what is said to you. Improv is about character change. The characters need to journey together, be changed by revelations, feel the impact of their choices, and be moved by emotional moments.

Just try it. Apply these guidelines to your situation. Notice how powerfully it registers with the other person and helps you advance through the uncertainty.

Improvisation is too good to leave to chance.
—**Paul Simon**

Let Intention
Guide You.

The future may be shrouded in uncertainty, but that doesn't mean you have to be aimless as you move through the fog. You're free to decide what *you* want . . . where *you* wish to go . . . how *you* would like for this to end up. This is your life story and you play the leading role, so help shape the plot!

Without a sense of direction, you'll wander. If you're not pursuing a specific end or destination, you're going to drift. So the cornerstone of your strategy should be to give yourself a sharp aiming point—a clear intention. GE's Jack Welch explained it this way: "In real life, strategy is actually very straightforward. Pick a general direction and implement like hell." So think deeply and decide what you want to see happen.

To get clear on this intention that will guide you through the uncertainty, quit obsessing about the factors that lie beyond your control. Stop fretting about all the ambiguity that blurs your visibility into the future. Take a break from your worries and frustrations about the obstacles that seem to block your way.

For now, just clear your mind so you can listen to your heart. Give your deepest self a chance to say what you want, what you're passionate about, what you will commit to quietly pursue in your thoughts and deeds. Keep this aiming point at the front of your consciousness. Bring it to life in your imagination. Finally, move yourself in that direction, easily but steadily, as opportunity presents itself.

This intention will serve as your North Star, helping you maintain your bearings as you maneuver through uncertainty. Just as important, and far more mysterious, is the power it has to pull you toward your aiming point.

Intention does more than serve as a compass . . . it works like a magnet.

As for the Future, your task is not to foresee, but to enable it.
—Antoine de Saint-Exupéry

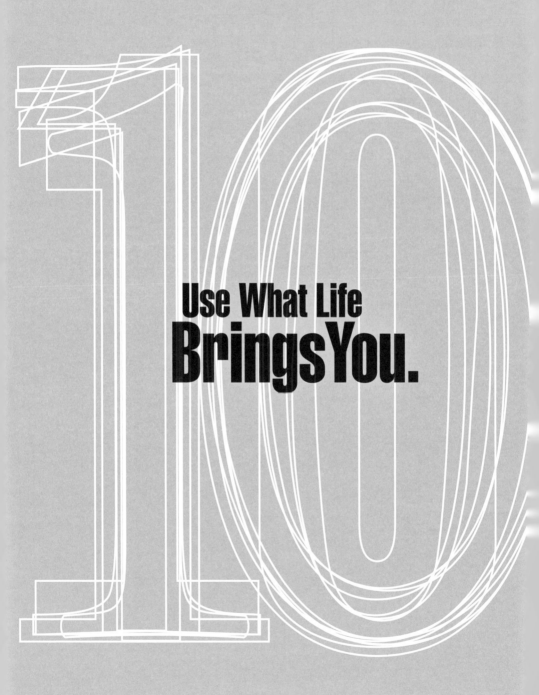

10

Use What Life Brings You.

So often people wait idly to see what will come of uncertainty. Their natural reflex is to sideline themselves, seeking refuge in passivity, presuming that they are best served by delaying action until the situation clears.

You might look at it differently.

What if you perceived this uncertainty as being here to serve a purpose? What if it has arrived in your life right on schedule? What if it holds possibilities far more promising than the path you've been traveling . . . *if* you're willing to use the moment?

Rather than wishing it away or hoping to just wait it out, you could choose to maneuver into the bank of fog with a hopeful spirit. You could consider this a unique window of opportunity that has opened in your life. Why not explore the mysteries? What sort of future might you now have a chance to shape if only you'll nudge yourself to *move*?

The great psychologist Alfred Adler said, "Trust only movement. Life happens at the level of events, not of words. Trust movement."

But perhaps you don't trust yourself to make the *right* moves.

Lee Iacocca's words might be helpful to you here: "So what do we do? Anything. Something. So long as we don't just sit there. If we screw it up, start over. Try something else. If we wait until we've satisfied all the uncertainties, it may be too late."

Life is like that, you know.

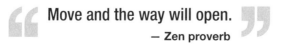

Move and the way will open.
— **Zen proverb**

BOOKS *by* PRITCHETT, LP

CHANGE MANAGEMENT

The 4ᵗʰ Level of Change: 10 Practices for Top Performance During Global Uncertainty

Business As UnUsual: The Handbook for Leading and Managing Organizational Change

The Employee Handbook for Organizational Change

The Employee Handbook of New Work Habits for a Radically Changing World: 13 Ground Rules for Job Success

Firing Up Commitment During Organizational Change

Hard Optimism: How to Succeed in a World Where Positive Wins

MindShift: The Employee Handbook for Understanding the Changing World of Work

Resistance: Moving Beyond the Barriers to Change

A Survival Guide to the Stress of Organizational Change

The Unfolding: A Handbook for Living Strong, Being Effective, and Knowing Happiness During Uncertain Times

GROWTH & INNOVATION

The Breakthrough Principle of 16x: Real Simple Innovation for 16 Times Better Results

Fast Growth: A Career Acceleration Strategy

The Mars Pathfinder Approach to "Faster-Better-Cheaper"

The Quantum Leap Strategy

you²: A High-Velocity Formula for Multiplying Your Personal Effectiveness in Quantum Leaps

CORPORATE CULTURE

Culture Shift: The Employee Handbook for Changing Corporate Culture

Shaping Corporate Culture: The Mission Critical Approach to Culture Integration and Culture Change

High-Velocity Culture Change: A Handbook for Managers

LEADERSHIP & TEAMWORK

Carpe Mañana: 10 Critical Leadership Practices for Managing Toward the Future

Deep Strengths: Getting to the Heart of High Performance

The Leadership Engine Handbook: Building Leaders at Every Level

Team ReConstruction: Building a High-Performance Work Group During Change

Teamwork: The Team Member Handbook

MERGERS & ACQUISITIONS

After the Merger: The Authoritative Guide for Integration Success

The Employee Guide to Mergers and Acquisitions

Making Mergers Work: A Guide to Managing Mergers and Acquisitions

Mergers: Growth in the Fast Lane

Smart Moves: A Crash Course on Merger Integration Management

OTHER

The Comeback

The Ethics of Excellence

Improving Performance: How to Manage the White Space on the Organizational Chart

Managing Sideways: Using the Rummler-Brache Process Improvement Approach to Achieve Breakthrough Performance

Outsourced: 12 New Rules for Running Your Career in an Interconnected World

Service Excellence!

Solution #1: The Handbook for Workplace Fitness and Health

Topgrading: How to Hire, Coach, and Keep A Players

What's Next? The Hard Core Truth About How to Get Hired

For information regarding PRITCHETT's training, keynotes, and consulting built around our handbooks, please call 800-992-5922.

Muscle up
the handbook's message!

Use our *Hacking Uncertainty* Power Tools and Training Sessions to help your people apply the 10 counterintuitive steps.

▶ Keep your people engaged during disruption and change
▶ Protect productivity
▶ Encourage creativity and innovation
▶ Reduce the stress of uncertainty
▶ Develop a more resilient work force

For information about content,
structure, and pricing,
call 800-992-5922 or visit
www.pritchettnet.com/uncertainty

ORDER ADDITIONAL COPIES OF

1-49 copies	$7.95 each
50-99 copies	$7.50 each
100-999 copies	$6.95 each
1,000-4,999 copies	$6.75 each
5,000-9,999 copies	$6.50 each
10,000 or more copies	$6.25 each

www.pritchettnet.com
or call
800-992-5922

Same-day shipping available

About the
Author

Price Pritchett grew up on a farm out
in the flat plains of West Texas some
80 miles south of Amarillo. He says,
"Mother Nature ran the place. We just
farmed it. The weather out there is so
unpredictable. I grew up in the arms
of uncertainty."

Having mastered the art of plowing with John Deere tractors by the age of
nine, he went on to earn B.A. and M.A. degrees in English, then a Ph.D. in
psychology. But he says his lessons from the farming life remain his best teach-
ings to this day, adding, "That's really where I learned how to live straight
into uncertainty."

Today Dr. Pritchett is recognized worldwide as an expert on personal and
organizational change. His firm's specialized work in change management,
corporate culture, and merger integration has been referenced in most of the
major business journals and newspapers. He also has been featured on CNN,
CNBC, and other major television channels. With over 20 million of his
books in print worldwide, he is one of the best-selling business authors in the
world. Virtually all of the Fortune 500 companies have used some combina-
tion of PRITCHETT's consulting, training, and publications.

HIS 30+ BOOKS AND HANDBOOKS HAVE
MORE THAN 20 MILLION COPIES IN PRINT,
MAKING HIM ONE OF THE BEST-SELLING
BUSINESS AUTHORS IN THE U.S.